Bear Runs for Office

Bear Runs for Office

Written by

Ken Stauffer

Illustrated by

Emily O'Shea

gatekeeper press
TAMPA, FLORIDA

The content associated with this book is the sole work and responsibility of the author. Gatekeeper Press had no involvement in the generation of this content.

Bear Runs for Office

Published by Gatekeeper Press

7853 Gunn Hwy., Suite 209
Tampa, FL 33626

www.GatekeeperPress.com

Copyright © 2024 by Ken Stauffer and Emily O'Shea

All rights reserved. Neither this book, nor any parts within it may be sold or reproduced in any form or by any electronic or mechanical means, including information storage and retrieval systems, without permission in writing from the author. The only exception is by a reviewer, who may quote short excerpts in a review.

ISBN (paperback): 9781662946189

Bear was very popular in his neighborhood.

Everyone wanted to say hi to him and he loved it!

One day Bear thought, "I would make a great 'Pet Mayor'."

So, he decided to run for office.

Bear asked his best dog-friend, Ziggy, to help him.

They talked to all the dogs in the neighborhood – Kyly, Jack, Bailey, and Attila.

Then all the dogs got busy stuffing messages in every doggy mailbox.

Max, the grumpy cat, heard Bear was running for office and asked,

"Can cats vote also?"

Bear and Ziggy didn't know what to say.

Cats are so different from dogs!

Cats look different,
play different,
eat different food,
and dogs often chase cats!

"Even if cats look different, they are pets.

And cats and dogs can live together in peace", Max said.

"People do have cats as pets", Bear reminded Ziggy.

"We should not exclude cats, just because they are different".

On election day, every pet in the neighborhood came to vote – not just cats and dogs!

Bear won "Pet Mayor" because he was truly a friend to all pets!

Ziggy became "Assistant Pet Mayor".

They asked Max, the grumpy cat, if he wanted to join their team.

But Max was just happy he had changed their minds about pets!

Even if some animals don't look and act like you, they are still pets and you can all be friends!

Bear's Bio

photo by Megan Stauffer

Bear is a Cockapoo; he is a mix of Cocker Spaniel and Poodle who was rescued from Best Friends Forever (BFF) in Brick New Jersey. His parents are Ken and Carol Stauffer, who adopted him at 7 months of age. He lives in his home by Silver Bay, New Jersey, and loves to play with his toys, go walking in the neighborhood, go boating and swimming – but his favorite past time is playing with his best buddy, Ziggy. Bear is also in the Bright and Beautiful Dog Therapy Program and visits several neighborhood hospitals weekly where he cheers up patients, doctors, and nurses.

Ziggy's Bio

Ziggy is a Sato living in Brick, NJ with his fur-parents Kyle and Megan Stauffer. Born in Puerto Rico, Ziggy was rescued when he was just a few weeks old and brought back to New Jersey by BFF Dog Rescue. Since his adoption, Ziggy spends his days running around the yard, going for long walks, and stealing his fur-parents socks. Ziggy also goes for swims and gets in trouble with his partner-in-crime, Bear. Even though Ziggy has had a few surgeries and physical therapy for his legs, it hasn't seemed to slow him down yet!

Ken Stauffer's Bio

Ken Stauffer was an electronics engineer who also decided to write children's books about his dog, Bear. Ken was born and raised in Tanzania; East Africa then came to the US at age 13. He worked as a stage manager in the professional theatre, as a researcher / developer at Bell Labs, and then became an entrepreneur in 1999, co-founding several companies and serving as CEO for 15 years. Ken really enjoys showing off Bear's winning personality in his books and as a therapy dog.

Emily O'Shea's Bio

Emily O'Shea is a multimedia designer who specializes in visual design and illustration. She has illustrated several children's books including "Maisy May and the Kittens" and "Bear Learns to Play Alone" and loves working on her own personal illustrations with a focus on animals and the natural world. Aside from her illustration work, Emily is currently working in the graphic design industry with a focus on motion graphics and animation.

www.ingramcontent.com/pod-product-compliance
Lightning Source LLC
LaVergne TN
LVHW071733060526
838200LV00031B/483